OptimaLearning®

Spanish For Kids™

For ages 2¹/₂–15

Learn Along With Your Child

To all those who believed like the little blue engine:

"I think I can, I think I can ...
I thought I could, I thought I could."

With special acknowledgement to Dr. Georgi Lozanov for his courageous and pioneering work in the field of accelerated learning, and to Dr. Ivan Barzakov for his vision and his special contributions in the field of mind development.

Special thanks to all those who helped to produce OptimaLearning SPANISH FOR KIDS :

Music and Lyrics	Erika Luckett and Jackie Rago
Carmen	Valentina Torres
Santiago	Santiago Portilla
Ana	Erika Luckett
Rosa	Jackie Rago
Dialogues	Pamela Rand
Translations	Jackie Rago, Elizabeth Wall
Sound Engineer	Dédé
Phonetic Symbols System	Elizabeth Wall
Artist	Shauna Lazazzero
Methodology Consultant	Ivan Barzakov, Ph. D.
Bilingual Consultant	Juan Benjumea, Meoy Gee
Consultants	Jorge Lerma
Editing, Typesetting	Juan Benjumea
Producer	Pamela Rand

About our musicians:

Erika Luckett was born in Mexico where she began playing the guitar at age 5. She has also lived in Brazil and Columbia. A gifted singer, musician and linguist, Erika is a graduate of the prestigious Berklee School of Music in Boston.

Jackie Rago's musical career began at the age of 4 in her native Venezuela. She is a classically trained mandolin player. In SPANISH FOR KIDS, she plays the Venezuelan Cuatro (a four string instrument), the Tres from Cuba, the mandolin and all percussion instruments.

In SPANISH FOR KIDS, Erika and Jackie introduce a wide range of rhythms. You will hear a Cuban Son in "Buenas Dias," a Brazilian Bossa Nova in "El Cuerpo" and a Ranchera from Mexico in "Los Animales."

CONTENTS

Cassettes

Instruction Cassette - **Red Label**
        Side 1   Lessons 1 - 5, Songs and Dialogues
        Side 2   Lessons 6 - 10, Songs and Dialogues

Reinforcement Cassette - **Green Label**
        Side 1   Songs only
        Side 2   Songs only, Supplementary Vocabulary (*terms of endearment, praises, commands, polite forms, useful expressions*)

CDs

Tracks 1-8   Lessons 1-8
Tracks 9-10   Lesson 9
Track 11   Lesson 10
Tracks 12-21 Reinforcement - review (Songs only)
Tracks 22-26 Supplementary Vocabulary with Baroque music (*terms of endearment, praises, commands, polite forms, useful expressions*)

INTRODUCTION

Congratulations on choosing this OptimaLearning® course for your child. This gift of early exposure to another language will build a wonderful foundation for language learning for both you and your child. Your child will have greater success in school and more opportunity at work in a global economy, if he or she can speak another language.

Why You Should Begin Exposing Your Young Child to Other Languages

Recent studies clearly show that the earlier you expose a child to several languages, the greater the child's mental development. Verbal skills, comprehension, and self-confidence are significantly enhanced. This special way of fostering both self-expression and the capabilities for language promotes future academic achievement.

Before your children can speak a language, they must be able to *hear* the particular sounds and auditory frequencies of that language, according to Dr. Alfred Tomatis (world-famous otolaryngologist and psychophysiologist). From the womb through early childhood, youngsters have a wide open sensitivity to a range of sounds. They quickly assimilate the accents, inflections and sound patterns of any language to which they are exposed. By the time children enter kindergarten, they know most of the grammar of their native tongue and its daily vocabulary. During this natural language development period, children quickly and joyfully pick up any language without conscious effort. Language permeates their activities.

During these early years, before the tongue and ear are conditioned completely to the sounds of English, a child can easily imitate the sounds of other languages, which many adults find difficult. Children's minds actually remember language in a different manner before the age of twelve, when biological changes in the brain make learning languages as difficult as it is for adults.

Neuron development in the brain is critical in a child's pre-school years. Stimulation develops neuron networks which in turn largely determine the child's ultimate physiological brain capacity. When children learn a second and third language, they are actually increasing their cognitive flexibility, a key to problem solving and creativity.

Dr. Tomatis demonstrated that *hearing* a language correctly is the most critical skill in language and learning development. Once children acquire this ability to hear the full range of another language, this capacity *remains* even if that language is unspoken for many years. When children begin formal study of that language in school, they retain the ability to speak with native intonation and accent, and are considered "gifted" in learning the language.

The Advantage of OptimaLearning's Spanish For Kids

You do not have to speak Spanish in order to share this special learning experience with your child or class. Incorporating the OptimaLearning method, this course is designed to allow even the non-Spanish speaking parent or caregiver to teach the lessons correctly and confidently. The written text is presented in three forms: Spanish, simple phonetics, and English. The recorded text and songs are all clearly delivered by fluent Spanish speakers so that your child will hear the language spoken accurately. You can relax and learn together with your child in a fun and easy way.

Each lesson is carefully designed for the young child with an interesting conversation, a short rhythmical song, and vocabulary that the child will understand and enjoy. The songs and dialogues are written and recorded by Erika Luckett and Jackie Rago. They are accompanied by 7 year old Valentina Torres and 9 year old Santiago Portilla. All are native Latin American speakers.

The following concise instructions introduce

you to the OptimaLearning method and describe how to set up an ideal learning environment for your child. There are suggested activities for each lesson, along with extra vocabulary, and a suggested toy or other object that can enhance the learning process.

The **red-labeled cassette** delivers the individual lessons. The **green-labeled cassette** presents the songs without dialogue, to provide a recreational reinforcement of the lessons. The **green-labeled cassette** contains supplementary vocabulary, introduced through a specialized accelerated learning technique of Reading with Music™.

Although designed for youngsters ages 2¹/2–8, this course can be enjoyed by children up to 15 years old and adults of any age. If you have older children at home who want to learn Spanish, you can enlist their help in teaching the younger ones. They can teach the new language while increasing self-confidence in their ability to learn the language at the same time.

Many mothers expose their newborns and, in some instances, their unborn infants, to the sounds and songs. Studies show that the fetus begins to "hear" sounds of the mother's voice at four months. This early exposure helps stimulate the brain and create optimal conditions for future mental development and ear training.

BEFORE YOU START

Before you begin, carefully review the following guiding principles and concepts of OptimaLearning. Become familiar with these principles. Think about how you can apply them in other ways in your parenting, caregiving, or teaching.

OptimaLearning® Environment and Ritual

Create a special OptimaLearning environment for these language sessions. This environment should be intimate, pleasant, and warm—a space where your child feels very comfortable. Select a place that has minimal distractions, such as a corner of a room or an area on the floor with the tape recorder nearby. If you choose the floor, you may want to use pillows for you and your child.

Another essential feature of the OptimaLearning environment is the *symbol*. This symbol could be a flag, a special doll, or some other item that symbolizes for you the culture of the new language (without being associated with any particular lesson). The symbol also serves as a signal that the session is about to begin, and helps the child and you to "shift" to another world. It should be put away at the end of each lesson.

Creating a special place and a ritual around the beginning of a learning activity helps the learner to mentally and physically make the transition to learning or working, and to retain the information longer and with easier recall. When you are away from home, be sure and take the symbol with you to maintain the link with the established ritual. As Dr. Ivan Barzakov, internationally recognized educational psychologist and expert in mind development says, "Encourage in your child ritualistic associations with the OptimaLearning environment which invoke the joy of learning."

Another aspect of the ritual is called the "alerting technique™," which aids the child in any transition. You "alert" your child whenever you give him/her a signal that you plan to change the activity. For instance, "When you finish eating, we're going for a walk." Or, "When you finish drawing that picture, we're going to listen to Carmen and Santiago." By alerting your child, rather than interrupting his or her activity with an immediate command, you give the child a few brief moments to complete an activity and prepare for a new one. The ritual itself should help build anticipation and excitement about the upcoming language lesson.

OptimaLearning is fun. If you need to get materials or arrange something for the OptimaLearning environment, or for the suggested activities of a particular lesson, enthusiastically invite your child to help. "Let's get our pillows so we can listen to Carmen and Santiago." "Come and help me draw for our Spanish lesson." After a while you may want to begin speaking in Spanish as you make the transition.

Remember to build anticipatory pleasure by reinforcing the child's competence and accomplishment. "You're learning so many new names for your face. Isn't it fun?" Or, "I love to hear you sing. Shall we learn a new song today in Spanish?"

PRINCIPLES AND CONCEPTS OF OPTIMALEARNING®

Expectancy vs. expectation.

Expectations are your greatest enemies! Unconsciously, you will project them to your children, who will develop frustration and lose self-confidence when their learning occurs in a different pattern. As native speakers, we don't think about the word sequence of a sentence or the way we hold our tongue when pronouncing a word. These habits of thought and speech are assimilated over long exposure. When a child begins talking (between the ages of 1–3) he or she is bringing to the surface for the first time the result of hundreds of hours of listening, observing, and responding. When language activity begins, it accelerates at an amazing speed. But each child is individual in the pattern and sequence of his or her speech development.

Accept your child. Rather than forming expectations of a particular progress path, create for your child the sense of delight and expectancy to be found in talking in another language. Help your child get excited about learning.

Ritual.

As you recall, a ritual in this course is a specific action or object which always happens or appears at the same time (for example, at the beginning of a lesson, or at the very end). The significance of ritual and how to establish it is outlined under *OptimaLearning Environment and Ritual* on page 2. Another example of "alerting" is to take your child on your lap for a special hug and a quiet moment just before starting the lesson. Be creative and think of a ritual that fits your child. For an older child, you might both try closing your eyes as you narrate a brief magic carpet ride to Mexico or Venezuela. Children love imaginative journeys.

Rhythm and Intonation.

Music has several special functions in OptimaLearning. The melody and rhythm provide an enriched framework for the memory. Children's songs are replete with repetition that aids learning as it provides a sense of the familiar. In this series, specially created songs will help your children learn and effortlessly practice new vocabulary. The clear voices of the singers and special rhythmical accompaniment is especially effective in accelerating the learning process.

Your own voice is also an instrument. Listen to its quality. Is it gentle and tender, inviting? Do you vary the pitch and timbre to create suspense and drama in conversation, as well as in story-telling? In creating an atmosphere of playful, happy learning, use your voice appropriately.

Educative Feedback™.

One of the keys to stress-free learning is Educative Feedback. The purpose of feedback in any system is to change future output. Feedback is neutral, non-judgmental and addresses performances, not the person. Thus, it is fundamentally different from criticism or correction in human relationships.

Educative Feedback differs from feedback in general through its special emphasis on building a sense of self-confidence. In language learning this can be achieved through the technique of "layering," along with ample support. "Layering" means that you will not directly interrupt or correct your child or children when they make mistakes. Instead you will encourage their responses in the new language and find an opportunity to substitute a better (more appropriate) model *without* labeling or calling attention to error. Remember to always encourage the child's expression and participation, no matter how unsatisfactory it appears according to your criteria. When supported and encouraged, your child will be very quick to adjust to the "correct" pronunciation.

Receptivity.

Learning is optimal when all levels of the mind are open and receptive to what is taught. This occurs when learners are excited, encouraged, and accepted. Several components of the OptimaLearning method help create these conditions of receptivity. As we discussed, these are expectancy, ritual, rhythm, intonation, and especially Educative Feedback.

A few additional tips:

Relax and let the tapes provide the initial models in the OptimaLearning course. As you

3

feel comfortable, engage in verbal exercises with your child. Don't be inhibited by your own lack of knowledge or fluency in the new language.

Avoid memorization. You did not learn your primary language through memorization. Exposure is the key. Your child is a natural language learner. Don't turn a lesson into a drill. Touch on the points and move on. There is always another opportunity. Meanwhile, don't underestimate the unseen learning that precedes spoken words.

Flow with your child's own pattern of learning. Use all the senses. Encourage your child to touch, move, look, sing, speak, even taste.

HOW TO USE THIS COURSE

- Familiarize yourself with our simple phonetic system to assist you with pronunciation. Take it easy. Don't be overly thorough – in time your mind will absorb everything. As Dr. Georgi Lozanov, psychiatrist, educator and father of modern accelerated learning says, "Allow a certain amount of the information to come through unconscious learning." Above all, be gentle with yourself, and playful – no one is going to test you.
- Create an OptimaLearning environment with all its components.
- Preview each new lesson before going over it with your child.
- Read over the appropriate Activities page or box of each lesson and gather the necessary materials for the exercises you choose that day. Whenever appropriate, prepare the optional object as a prop for that lesson.

Your preparation is now complete.

BASIC LESSON SEQUENCE

ADVANCE the **red**-labeled cassette to the lesson you are studying.

INVITE your child to learn, and build expectancy (as previously described).

OPEN the book to the appropriate lesson to follow along while you play it on the tape recorder.

LISTEN to the short dialogue. Point to the picture to help your child make connections. For example, in the Mariposa (Butterfly) song, all the insects, birds and other nouns are named.

TURN off the tape recorder and engage your child in the suggested activities for the day.

The sequence may take 5 to 20 minutes depending on the age of the learner and how much activity you choose to do.

Then, turn the tape recorder back on to hear the recorded lesson again.

Reinforce the lessons with the **green** labeled cassette at home or in the car, and at night before going to sleep.

How Often?

Try to have your OptimaLearning language sessions once a day at about the same time. Repeat a lesson several times before going on to the next lesson. Then review it 3 or 4 days later, and at least twice during the following week. You are not trying to achieve mastery, just exposure, the first time through the course.

You're now ready to progress to the next level, or you can begin this cycle again, depending upon your child and how much Spanish he or she is able to speak at this time. If your child is not yet speaking Spanish or speaking very little, the continued review will be extremely beneficial.

If your child has memorized all the songs and dialogues and has begun to respond verbally to questions, keep using the language by reviewing and expanding activities. Listen to the tapes and dialogues as old family friends and favorite stories. Children love repetition, especially when they can actively participate in singing or telling the story.

The OptimaLearning sequence should be followed for each lesson. Depending on your child's attention span, you may extend periods of play and improvisation, but always quit before your child is tired or bored.

Easy Does It !!

Above all, just as you wouldn't push your child, don't push yourself. The procedures in this workbook are designed for optimal results, but you may skip some of them if you don't feel motivated to do it all. OptimaLearning should be fun for both your child *and you*.

Listening is the first step in learning a language. Help your child become an active listener by showing your excitement and interest in the songs and dialogues. Let your face register emotion – wonderment, surprise, delight. As soon as possible, join in singing the songs as you learn them. Encourage your child to sing as well. As soon as a song is learned, sing it anywhere during the day, at home, and play the **green** labeled cassette (songs only) in the car. An ideal time for absorption and retention is in the so-called "twilight zone," in bed just before going to sleep, and right after waking.

Response to language is the next step in a child's learning. According to James Asher (author of *Total Physical Response*), you should let your child become physically involved before seeking verbal responses. For instance, point to the pictures, reach for the sun, enact the greeting process. The second lesson involves a kitty and a dog. Have your child pet a soft stuffed or real animal and hold it during the dialogue.

In the activities you can become as imaginative and playful as possible. Don't rush the child. Enjoy the absurd. Encourage laughter. Involving the total physical response is a key way we teach our children their native language, and it is especially effective for children learning a new language. Use the principles of OptimaLearning: acceptance, expectancy, rhythm and intonation, receptivity, and Educative Feedback.

Language learning for children and increased memory comes through repeated exposure from different angles and perspectives, according to research by Georgi Lozanov and Ivan Barzakov, and confirmed by studies of Karl Pribram, world-renowned neuroscientist, and Michael S. Gazzaniga, pioneering brain researcher and psychologist. Don't push your child to memorize – avoid struggle! Just continue to provide language exposure in regular, stress-free, playful environments.

We invite you to report your experiences to OptimaLearning Language Land™ (885 Olive Avenue, Suite A, Novato, CA 94945). We want to know how your child responded and what worked well for you.

¡Buen Viaje!

A Little Bit About Spanish Pronunciation.

Spanish is spoken in many different countries. Each of these countries has its own culture, its own traditions, and its own **accent**. Here in the United States, these all seem to get mixed up as immigrants interact with other Spanish speaking people. Still, you can hear the difference between, say, a Mexican's and a Colombian's Spanish. We have tried to present a South American as "generic" as possible. We think you will find it quite fascinating to hear these slight differences in pronunciation. You may hear one child pronounce, for instance, the word for rain - <u>lluvia</u> like joobee-a and the other says yoobee-a. Or one child will put more stress on the end of a word than the other.

Think for a moment how people in other regions of the United States speak for that matter, try listening to an Australian or an Irish person for an hour or so. In fact, you might consider discussing this phenomenon with your child. It is amazing what insights little people have when you help them to dig deep into their creative minds!

The other major point we would like to make about Spanish is that it follows the rules. Unlike English which tells you that a letter should sound a certain way and then changes its mind for no apparent reason. (Why do we say "bowl" is *bol*, but "howl" is *howl*?).

Just remember a few simple rules:

(1)   **C** changes from a K sound to an S sound before E or I
      cada   *kada*   each   /   cielo   *seeyelo*   sky

(2)   **G** changes from a G sound to an H sound before E or I
      tengo   *tengo*   I have   /   gente   *henteh*   people

(3)   When two vowels sounds are together they retain their individual sounds. Thus, **AI** becomes a-ee and **AU** becomes a-oo (or try saying ow).
      bailar   *bailar*   to dance   /   aplaudir   *aplowdeer*   to clap

(4)   **H** is silent in Spanish
      ahora   *a-ora*   now

(5)   **J**, the soft **G**, and sometimes **X** make a sound a little deeper than our English H sound.
      jabón   *habon*   soap   /   gente   *henteh*   people
      Mexico   *Meheeko*   Mexico

(6)   When **E** shows up at the end of a word, like madre (mother), it tends to sound like *ay*, but try not to drag it out so much. We are using the phonetic *eh*, to remind you not to say *ay*.
      grande   *grandeh*   big (large)

(7)   **RR** is a funny sound to pronounce, and everyone will try to tell you their trick for a rolled R. If you can purr like a cat, then you might as well try our trick. We say that the RR is like a "purrrr" with your voice behind it.
      barrer   *barrer*   to sweep

Well, you're off on an exciting adventure with your family. You are opening new doors and widening horizons.

Especially remember to have fun!

Pronunciation Guide

One Letter Sounds

Spanish	Sound		Phonetic		Spanish	Sound		Phonetic	
A	a	**a**ño	anyo	year	N	n	**n**ada	nada	nothing
B	b	**b**oca	boka	mouth	Ñ	ny	**ni**ña	neenya	girl
C	k or s	**c**ada	cada	each	O	o	**o**rar	orar	to pray
D	d	**d**os	dos	two	P	p	**p**ato	pato	duck
E	e or eh	**e**st**e**	esteh	this	Q	k	**qu**e	keh	what
F	f	**f**ruta	froota	fruit	R	r	**r**osa	rosa	rose
G	g or h	**g**ato	gato	cat	S	s	**s**ol	sol	sun
H	_	**h**acer	acer	to do/make	T	t	**t**omar	tomar	to take
I	ee	**i**r	eer	to go	U	oo	**lu**z	loos	light
J	h	**j**ugo	hugo	juice	V	b	**v**er	ber	to see
K	k	**k**ilo	keelo	kilogram	X	h	Mé**x**ico	meheeko	Mexico
L	l	**l**indo	leendo	pretty	Y	y or ee	**y**o	yo	I
M	m	**m**ano	mano	hand	Z	s	**z**apato	sapato	shoe

Two Letter Sounds

Spanish	Sound		Phonetic	
CH	ch	**ch**ulo	choolo	handsome
LL	y	**ll**uvia	yoobee-a	rain
RR	rr	co**rr**er	korrer	to run
AI	ai	b**ai**lar	bailar	to dance
AU	ow	apl**au**dir	aplowdeer	clap
AY	ai	h**ay**	ai	there is
OY	oy	h**oy**	oy	today

Consonants Sounds

Sound	Is like...		Sound	Is like...
B	boy		N	nut
K	kite		P	park
D	dog		R	rain
F	friend		S	sun
G	girl		T	toy
H	(see note 4)		W	window
L	lamb		Y	yo-yo
M	mother			

Vowels Sounds

Sound	Is Like...
A	father
AI	(see note 3)
AY	day
E	pet
EE	sleep
EH	(see note 6)
O	hello
OO	moon
OW	cow
OY	boy

BUENOS DÍAS
bwenos dee-as
Good morning

Buenos días, buenos días.
¡Muy buenos días tenga usted!
bwenos dee-as, bwenos dee-as
moo-ee bwenos dee-as tenga usted
Good morning, good morning.
Have a very good morning!

Buenos días ...

Saludo a la mañana. Saludo al cielo azul.
A los pajaritos, ¿y a quién saludas tú?
saloodo a la manyana saloodo al seeyelo asool
a los pahareetos   ee a kyen saloodas too
Hello to the morning. Hello to the blue sky.
To the birds and to whom do you say hello to?

Buenos días ...

Saludo a mi mamá. Saludo a mi papá.
A mis amiguitos y a todos los demás.
saloodo a mee mama saloodo a mee papa
a mees ameegeetos ee a todos los demass
Hello to my mom.   Hello to my dad.
To my friends   and all   the   others.

Buenos días ...

Saludo al sol brillante.
    Saludo a los colores.
A los animalitos y a todas las flores.
saloodo al sol breeyanteh
    saloodo a los kolores
a los aneemaleetos ee a todas las flores
Hello to the bright sun.
    Hello to the colors.
To the animals and to all the flowers.

¡Buenos días amiguitos! Buenos días.
bwenos dee-as ameegeetos
Good morning my little friends.

¡Les saludo! Buenos días.
Les saloodo!
I say hello to you!

¡Hola amiguitos! Buenos días.
ola ameegeetos
Hi   friends!

¡A la tierra! Buenos días.
a la tee-era
To the earth!

¡Aquí, dame un besito! Buenos días.
akee dame oon beseeto
Here, come give me a kiss!

¡Abrázame! Buenos días.
abrasame
Hug me!

¡Te quiero mucho! Buenos días.
te kyero moocho
I love you a lot!

¡Al arco iris! Buenos días.
al arko eerees
To the rainbow!

¡Y a mi gatita! Buenos días.
ee a mee gateeta
And to my kitty!

¡A la mariposa! Buenos días.
ee la mareeposa
To the butterfly!

¡Te quiero mucho! Buenos días.
te kyero moocho
I love you very much

¡A los planetas! Buenos días.
a los planetas
To the planets!

¡Y al sapito! Buenos días.
¡Lo quiero mucho! Buenos días.
ee al sapeeto
lo kyero moocho
To the frog!
I love it very much!

¡Ay, buenos días! Buenos días.
ai bwenos dee-as.
Hey, good morning!

¡Tengan todos buenos días!
tengan   todos bwenos dee-as
Everyone have a good morning!

¡Y al planeta! Buenos días .
ee al planeta
And to the planet!

¡Y a mis juguetes! Buenos días .
ee a mees hoogetes
And to my toys!

¡Al sol brillante! Buenos días .
al sol breeyanteh
To the shining sun!

¡Y a las nubes! Buenos días .
ee a las noobes
And to the clouds!

DIALOGUE

Santiago, Carmen, Ana

A: ¡Hola! ¿Cómo te llamas?
    ola   komo te yamas
    Hi!   What is your name?

C: Yo me llamo Carmen.
    yo me yamo karmen
    My name is Carmen.

A: ¡Hola Carmen!
    ola karmen
    Hi Carmen.

C: ¿Cómo te llamas?
    komo te yamas
    What is your name?

A: Mi nombre es Ana.
      ¿Y tú, como te llamas?
    mee nombreh es ana
      ee too komo te yamas
    My name is Ana.
      And what is your name?

S: Yo me llamo Santiago.
yo me yamo santeeyago
My name is Santiago.

A: Ah, ya veo. ¿Carmen es tu hermana?
a ya bayo karmen es too ermana
I see. Is Carmen your sister?

S: No, ella no es mi hermana.
Ella es mi amiga.
no eya no es mee ermana
eya es mee ameega
No, she is not my sister.
She is my friend.

A: Carmen, ¿tienes algún
hermano o hermana?
karmen tyenes algoon
ermano o ermana
Carmen, do you have a
brother or a sister?

C: Sí, tengo un hermano y dos hermanas.
see tengo oon ermano ee dos ermanas
Yes, I have one brother and two sisters.

A: Y tú Santiago, ¿tienes
hermanos o hermanas?
ee too santeeyago tyenes
ermanos o ermanas
And you, Santiago, do you have
brothers or sisters?

S: No, no tengo ningún
hermano o hermana.
no no tengo neengoon
ermano o ermana,
No, I have no
brothers or sisters.

C: ¡Mira Ana!¡ Mira Santiago!
¿Quién es ese?
meera ana meera santeeyago
kyen es eseh
Look Ana! Look Santiago!
Who is that?

S: ¡Es un payaso! ¿Cómo se llama?
es oon payaso komo se yama
It's a clown! What's his name?

A: Se llama Pancho,
Pancho, el payaso.
se yama pancho
pancho el payaso
His name is Pancho,
Pancho the clown.

C: ¡Mira! ¿Qué tiene en las manos?
meera keh tyeneh en las manos
Look! What does he have in his hands?

S: Tiene uno...dos...tres... globos.
tyeneh oono dos tres globos
He has 1... 2 .... 3... balloons.

A: A mí me gustan los globos.
¿Y a ustedes * les gustan?
a mee me goostan los globos
ee a oostedes les goostan
I like balloons.
And you, do you like balloons?

S: Sí, a mí también me gustan los globos,
y me gusta jugar con ellos.
see a mee tambyen me goostan los globos
ee me goosta hoogar kon eyos
Yes, I also like balloons
and I like to play with them.

A: Y a mí me gusta cantar.
¿A ustedes les gusta cantar?
ee a mee me goosta kantar
a oostedes les goosta kantar
And me, I like to sing.
And you, do you like to sing?

C: Sí, a mí me encanta cantar.
see a mee me enkanta kantar
Yes, it makes me happy to sing.

S: A mí también.
a mee tambyen
I like to as well.(Me, too)

A: ¡Miren!
meeren
Look! (plural form)

S: ¿Qué es eso?
keh es eso
What is that?

A: Es mi guitarra.
¡Vamos a cantar juntos!
es mee geetarra
vamos a kantar hoontos
It's my guitar.
come on, let's sing together!

Buenos días ...
Buenos días ...

* Usted is the polite form of address. Ustedes is plural of Usted and Tú in Latin American Spanish.

9

GATITA
gateeta
Kitty

Yo tengo una gatita. Misú, Misú, Misú.
¡Qué linda mi gatita! Misú, Misú, Misú.
yotengo oona gateeta. meesoo, meesoo...
keh leenda mee gateeta
I have a little kitty. Misou, Misou, Misou.
How pretty, my little kitty!

¡Allá la veo pasar! ¡Corre, salta, brinca!
¡Juega aquí conmigo! ¿Gatita, dónde estás?
aya la bayo pasar   korre salta breenka
hwega akee konmeego   gateeta dondeh estas
There I see her pass by! She runs, jumps, hops!
Play here with me!   Kitty, where are you?

Miau, miau, miau. ¡Allá la veo pasar!
Miau, miau, miau. ¡Corre, salta, brinca!
Miau, miau, miau. ¡Juega aquí conmigo!
meeow meeow meeow
Miau, miau, miau.

Gatita, amiguita. ¿Gatita, dónde estás?
gateeta ameegeeta
Litte kitty, little friend.
Gatita, amiguita. ¿Gatita, dónde estás?

Yo tengo una gatita...
Yo tengo una gatita...

DIALOGUE

Santiago-Carmen
Miau, miau.

C: **¡Mira! Un gatito. Ven gatito, misú, misú, misú, misú.**
¿Cuáles es tu nombre?
meera oon gateeto ben gateeto meesoo meesoo...
kwal es too nombreh
Look! A kitten. Come here kitten. Kitty, kitty...
What is your name?

S: **Su nombre es Blanquita. Es una gatita.**
soo nombreh es blankeeta es oona gateeta
Her name is Blanquita. She is a girl kitten.

C: **¿La puedo acariciar?**
la pwedo akareesee-ar
Can I   pet her?

S: **Sí, pero suavemente.**
see pero swabementeh
Yes, but   gently.

C: **¡Qué cola tan linda y tan blanca!**
¿Y qué son estos? Miau, miau!!!!
keh kola tan leenda ee tan blanka
ee keh son estos
What a tail - so pretty and so white!
And what are these?

S: **Son sus bigotes. No se los jales.**
Ten cuidado, ella es muy delicada.
son soos beegotes no se los hales
ten kweedado eya es moo-ee deleekada
They are her whiskers. Don't pull them.
Be careful,   she is very delicate.

C: **Lo siento, Blanquita. ¿Te hice daño?**
Ummm... Qué suave eres, Blanquita.
lo seeyento blankeeta   te eeseh danyo
mmmm   keh swabeh eres   blankeeta
I'm sorry, Blanquita.   Did I hurt you?
Ummm... How soft you are, Blanquita.

C: **¡Ey! Blanquita, espera. No te vayas.**
No corras. ¿Dónde estás? ¿Aquí o allá?
ay blankeeta   espera   note bayas
no korras   dondeh estas   akee o aya
Hey! Blanquita, wait.   Don't go.
Don't run away. Where are you? Here or there?

C: **¡Un perrito! ¿De dónde vino?**
oon perreeto de dondeh beeno
A little dog! Where did he come from?

S: **Es mi perro. Se llama Lucho.**
es mee perro   seyama loocho
He's my dog. His name is Lucho.

C: **¿Lo puedo tocar? ¿Muerde?**
lo pwedo tokar   mwerdeh
Can I touch him? Does he bite?

S: **Sí, lo puedes tocar. El no muerde.**
see lo pwedes tokar   el no mwerdeh
Yes, you can touch him. He doesn't bite.

C: **¡Hola, Lucho! ¿Qué tal?**
¿Quieres ser mi amigo?
ola loocho   keh tal
kyeres ser mee ameego
Hi Lucho! How are you?
Do you want to be my friend?

C: **Me dice que sí.   Quiere ser mi amigo.**
meh deeseh keh see kyereh ser mee ameego
He says yes.   He wants to be my friend.

S: **Carmen, vámonos a jugar.**
karmen   bamonos a hoogar
Carmen,   let's go play.

C: **Vamos Santiago.**
bamos santeeyago
Let's go, Santiago.

LA MARIPOSA
la mareeposa
Butterfly

Vuela, vuela, mariposa. Vuela, vuela, ven a mí.
Con tus alitas abiertas, mariposa, ven a mí.
bwela bwela mareeposa   bwela bwela ben a mee
kon toos aleetas abee-ertas mareeposa ben a mee
Fly,   fly   Butterfly.   Fly, fly,   come to me.
With your little wings open, butterfly, come to me.

Tú bailas con las flores y vuelas sin parar.
Mariposa linda, amiguita, ven acá.
too bailas kon las flores ee bwelas seen parar
mareeposa leenda ameegeeta ben aka
You dance with the flowers and fly without stopping.
Beautiful butterfly, little friend, come here.

Mariposa linda, amiguita, ven acá.

Vuela, vuela, mariposa...

Vuelas en la montaña con muchos pajaritos.
Mariposa linda, mi amiga, ven aquí.
bwelas en la montanya kon moochos pahareetos
mareeposa leenda mee ameega ben akee
You fly in the mountain with many little birds.
Beautiful butterfly, my little friend, come here.
Mariposa linda, mi amiga, ven aquí.

Vuela, vuela, mariposa...

Ven, mariposita, para jugar conmigo.
Mariposa linda, amiguita, ven aquí.
ben mareeposeeta para hoogar konmeego
mareeposa leenda ameegeeta ben akee
Come butterfly to play with me.
Beautiful butterfly, little friend, come here.
Mariposa linda amiguita ven aquí.

Vuela, vuela, mariposa...

DIALOGUE

Ana - Santiago - Carmen

A: **¡Santiago, Carmen, vengan!**
Santeeyago karmen vengan
Santiago, Carmen, come here!

C: **¿Dónde estás, Ana?**
dondeh estas ana
Where are you, Ana?

A: **Estoy aquí en el jardín. Shhh. No hagas ruido.**
estoy akee en el hardeen shhh
no agas roo-eedo
I am here in the garden. shhh.
Don't make any noise.

C: **¿Por qué? ¿Qué es? ¿Un pájaro?**
por keh   keh es   oon paharo
Why?   What is it?   A bird?

A: **Es una mariposa grande. ¡Mira!**
es oona mareeposa grandeh meera
It's a   big butterfly.   Look!

C: **¡Ay, es tan linda!**
ai,   es tan leenda
Oh! it's (she) so beautiful!

S: **¿La puedo tocar?**
la   pwedo tokar
Can I touch it (her)?

A: **No. No la toques. Sólo vamos a verla.**
no   nola tokes   solo bamos a berla
No. Don't touch it (her.). We're only going to watch it.

C: **Mira sus alas. Se abren y se cierran.**
Se están moviendo.
meera soos alas se estan   mobeeyendo
se abren ee se syerran
Look at it's wings. They are moving
by themselves.
They open and close.

Bzzzzzzzz

S: **¿Oíste eso?**
o-eesteh eso
Did you hear that?

C: **Sí, es una mosca.**
see, es oona moska
Yes, it's a fly.

Abeja: **¡No soy una mosca! ¿No me ves? Soy una abeja. Bzzzz ¿Puedes hacer así? Bzzzzzz**
abeha   no soy oona moska   no me bes   soy oona abeha   bzzzz   puedes aser asee   bzzzz
Bee   I am not a fly!   Can't you see me? I'm a bee.   Bzzzz   Can you do this?   Bzzzzzzzz

S: **¡Qué divertido! Bzzzzzzz**
keh deeberteedo bzzzzzz
What fun!   Bzzzzzzz

Mosca: **Bzzzzzz ¡Hola! Soy la mosca.**
Moska   ola   soy la moska
Fly   Hi!   I'm the fly.

C: **¿Dónde vives? ¿En las montañas?**
¿Con los pájaros?
dondeh beebes   en las montanyas
kon los paharos
Where do you live? In the mountains?
With the birds?

Abeja: **Vivimos aquí en este árbol grande.**
La mariposa, la mosca y yo.
beebeemos akee en esteh arbol grandeh
la   mareeposa la moska ee yo
We live   here in this big tree.
The butterfly,   the fly and I.

S: **¿Puedo volar contigo?**
pwedo   bolar konteego
Can I   fly with you?

C: **Santiago, tú no puedes volar. No tienes alas.**
santeeyago too no pwedes bolar no tyenes alas.
Santiago, you can't fly.   You don't have wings.

S: **Lo sé. Vamos a jugar a que yo soy la mosca y tú, Carmen, eres la abeja.**
lo seh bamos a hoogar a keh   yo soy la moska
ee too karmen eres la abeha.
I know. Let's pretend (play) that I'm the fly
and you, Carmen, are the bee.

Bzzzzzzzzzzzzzzzzzzzzzzzzzzzzzzzzzz

11

El SAPITO Y LA LLUVIA
el sapeeto ee la yoobee-a
The Little Frog and the Rain

¡Ojalá qué llueva! ¡Qué llueva! ¡Qué llueva!
ohala keh yweba keh yweba keh yweba
ohala keh yweba
Let it rain! Let it rain! Let it rain!
Let it rain!

Yo brinco, yo salto, me mojo los piecitos.
Está lloviendo mucho, Sapito Saltarón.
yo breenko yo salto me moho los pee-eseetos
esta yobee-endo moocho sapeeto saltaron
I hop, I jump, I get my little feet wet.
It's raining a lot little Jumping Frog.

Ojalá qué llueva...

Yo oigo, yo canto, las gotas van sonando.
Me siento muy contento, Sapito Saltarón.
yo oygo yo kanto las gotas ban sonando
me seeyento moo-ee kontento sapeeto saltaron
I listen, I sing, the drops make sounds.
I feel very happy, little Jumping Frog.

Plin, plin, plin, las gotas de la lluvia.
Ploc, ploc, ploc, los saltos del sapito.
Ja, ja, ja, la risa de los niños.
La, la, la, canta conmigo, Sapito Saltarón.
pleen pleen pleen las gotas de la yoobee-a
ploc ploc ploc los saltos del sapeeto
ha ha ha la reesa de los neenyos
la la la kanta konmeego sapeeto saltaron
Plin, plin, plin, the rain drops.
Ploc, ploc, ploc, the jumping of the frog.
Ha, ha, ha, the laughter of the children.
La, la, la, sing with me, little Jumping Frog.
Canta conmigo, Sapito Saltarón.

Ojalá qué llueva...
Plin, plin, plin ...
Ojalá qué llueva...

DIALOGUE

Santiago y Carmen

S: ¿Qué es ese ruido?
keh es eseh roo-eedo?
What is that noise?

C: No sé.
no seh
I don't know.

S: Vamos a ver qué es.
bamos a ber keh es
Let's go see what it is.

C: ¡Ay! ¡Mira! Es un sapito. ¿Lo ves?
ai meera es oon sapeeto lo bes
Wow! Look! It's a little frog. Do you see it?

S: Sí, lo veo. ¿Y por qué está agarrando una sombrilla?
see lo bayo ee por keh esta agarrando oona sombreeya
Yes, I see it. And why is he holding an umbrella?

C: Porque está lloviendo. ¿Puedes ver la lluvia?
porkeh esta yobee-endo pwedes ber la yoobee-a
Because it's raining. Can you see the rain?

S: Sí, veo las gotas de lluvia. ¿Cuántas hay?
see bayo las gotas de yoobee-a kwantas ai
Yes, I see the drops of rain. How many are there?

C: Uno, dos, tres, cuatro, cinco, seis, siete, ocho, nueve, diez...
oono dos tres kwatro seenko says seeyete ocho nwebe dyes ...
One, two, three, four, five, six, seven, eight, nine, ten...

S: Once, doce, trece, catorce y quince. Hay quince gotas.
onseh doseh treseh katorseh ee keenseh ai keenseh gotas
Eleven, twelve, thirteen, fourteen and fifteen. There are fifteen drops.

C: Plin, plin, plin.

S: Sí, me gusta sentir la lluvia en mis manos. Plin, plin, plin, siento las gotas.
see me goosta senteer la yoobee-a en mees manos pleen pleen pleen seeyento las gotas
Yes, I love to feel the rain in my hands. Plick, plick, plick, I feel the drops.

S: Me siento muy contento cuando llueve.
me seeyento moo-ee kontento kwando yvebe
I feel very happy when it rains.

S: Los sapitos saltan todo el día.
los sapeetos saltan todo el deeya
The little frogs jump all day long.

C: Yo también puedo saltar como un sapito.
yo tambyen pwedo saltar komo oon sapeeto
I also can jump like a little frog.

S: Está lloviendo mucho. Me estoy mojando.
esta yobee-endo moocho me estoy mohando
It's raining a lot. I am getting wet.

C: Me gusta mojarme.
me goosta moharmeh
I like to get wet.

S: A mí no. Vamos a correr hasta la casa. Tú saltas y yo brinco.
a mee no bamos a korrer asta la kasa too saltas ee yo breenko
Not me. Let's run up to the house. You jump and I'll hop.

C: Está bien. ¡En sus marcas, listos, fuera!
esta byen en soos markas leestos fwera
O.K. On your mark, get set, go!

ARCO IRIS
arko eerees
Rainbow

Arco iris, hay tantos colores. Arco iris, estás en todas partes. Arco iris, estás aquí y allá.
arko eerees ai tantos kolores   arko eerees estas en todas partes   arko eerees estas akee ee aya
Rainbow, there are so many colors. Rainbow, you're everywhere. Rainbow, you're here and there.

Arco iris, cuando miro al cielo. Arco iris, te veo allá. Arco iris, tan grande, mi amigo.
arko eerees kwando meero al seeyelo arko eerees te bayo aya arko eerees tan grande mee ameego
Rainbow, when I look at the sky. Rainbow, I see you there. Rainbow, (you're) so big, my friend.

¿Puedo tocarte? ¿Puedo abrazarte? Eres tan grande y tan bello, arco iris.
pwedo tokarte   pwedo abrasarte   eres tan grandeh ee tan bayo arko eerees
Can I touch you? Can I hug you? You're so big and so beautiful, rainbow.

Veo naranja, amarillo y rojo. Veo verde y azul. Veo colores, y te veo, arco iris.
bayo naranha amareeyo ee roho bayo berdeh y azool beo kolores y te bayo arko eerees
I see orange, yellow and red. I see green and blue. I see colors and I see you, rainbow.

Arco iris, montaré en tu cola.
arko-eerees montareh en too kola
Rainbow, I'll jump on your tail.

Arco iris, empujaremos (las) nubes.
arko eerees empooharemos (las) noobes
Rainbow, we'll push away clouds.

Andaremos con el viento y el sol.
andaremos kon el byento y el sol
We'll walk with the wind and the sun.

Arco iris, ¿serás mi amigo?
arko eerees seras mee ameego
Rainbow, will you be my friend?

Arco iris, jugaremos tanto. Arco iris, solamente tú y yo.
arko eerees hoogaremos tanto arko eerees solamente too ee yo
Rainbow, we'll play so much. Rainbow, just you and I.

¿Puedo tocarte?...
Arco iris, hay tantos colores...

DIALOGUE

Santiago, Carmen, Ana y el Arco Iris

C: **Arco iris, arco iris. ¡Es un arco iris!**
arko eerees arko eerees es oon arko eerees
Rainbow, rainbow! It's a rainbow!

S: **¡Es muy lindo!**
es moo-ee leendo
It's very pretty.

C: **Siempre sale   después que llueve.**
syempreh saleh   despwes keh ywebe
It always comes out after it rains.

S: **Sí, pero sólo si hay sol.**
see pero solo see ai sol
Yes, but only if there is sun.

C: **Sí, es verdad. Me olvidé del sol.**
see es berdad   me olveedeh del sol
Yes, it's true. I forgot about the sun.

S: **Hay tantos colores en el arco iris.**
ai tantos kolores   en el arko eerees
There are so many colors in the rainbow.

C: **Sí, veo el anaranjado, el amarillo, el rojo, el verde y el azul.**
see bayo el anaranhado el amareeyo el roho el berde ee el asool
Yes, I see orange, yellow, red, green and blue.

S: **También veo el morado y el blanco.**
tambyen bayo el morado y el blanko
I also see   purple and white.

C: **Mira, qué grande es el arco iris. Está en el cielo y en todas partes.**
meera keh grandeh es el arko eerees esta en el seeyelo ee en todas partes
Look, how big   the rainbow is.   It's in the sky and everywhere.

S: **¡Está aquí!**
esta akee
It's here!

C: **Y está allá.   ¿Puedo tocarlo?**
ee esta aya   pwedo tokarlo
And it's over there. Can I touch it?

S: **No, está muy lejos.**
no esta moo-ee lehos
No, it's very far away.

C: **Ya lo sé, pero sería muy divertido tocarlo. Dime, arco iris, ¿ puedo jugar contigo? ¿Me puedo montar en tu cola?**
ya lo seh pero sereea moo-ee deeverteedo tokarlo deemeh arko eerees pwedo hoogar konteego me pwedo montar en too kola
I know it, but it would be a lot of fun to touch it. Tell me, rainbow, can I play with you? Can I ride on your tail?

S: **No puedes porque el arco iris está allá arriba. Muy lejos...**
no pwedes porkeh el arko eerees esta aya arreeba moo-ee lehos
You can't because the rainbow is way up there. Very far away...

C: **Arco iris, ven.   Llévame contigo, por favor.**
arko eerees ben   yebame konteego por fabor
Rainbow, come here.   Take me with you, please.

AI: No, sería muy peligroso para ti. Aquí arriba hay mucho viento.
no sereeya moo-ee peleegroso para tee akee arreeba ai moocho beeyento
No, it would be very dangerous for you. Way up here, there is a lot of wind.

C: Pero arco iris yo quiero ser tu amiga.
pero arko eerees yo kyero ser too ameega
But rainbow, I want to be your friend.

A: Carmen, Santiago, vengan. Ya es hora de comer.
karmen santeeyago bengan ya es ora de komer
Carmen, Santiago, come. It's time to eat.

C: Está bien, arco iris. Me tengo que ir ahora. Vendré pronto. Tú eres mi amigo..
esta byen arko eerees me tengo keh eer a-ora bendreh pronto too eres mee ameego
O.K. rainbow, I have to go now. I'll come back soon. You're my friend.

S: Sí, arco iris, yo también soy tu amigo.
see arko eerees yo tambyen soy too ameego
O yes, rainbow, I'm also your friend.

AI: Hasta luego, amiguitos. Los veré después.
asta luego ameegeetos los bereh despwes
So long little friends. I'll see you later.

S, C: Adiós, arco iris.
adeeyos arko eerees
Goodbye rainbow.

14

COMER/BEBER
komer / beber
To Eat/To Drink

Comer, comer, a mí me gusta comer.
Me gustan las frutas. Me gustan los vegetales.
Como tres veces al día para que me de energía.
komer komer a mee me goosta komer
me goostan las frootas me gustan los vegetales
komo tres beses al dee-a para keh me de enerhee-a
Eat, eat, I like to eat.
I like fruit. I like vegetables.
I eat three times a day to give me energy.

Comer, comer, a mí me gusta comer...

Me siento a la mesa y me tomo la sopa. Luego
la ensalada. Y termino con la fruta.
me syento a la mesa ee me tomo la sopa lwego
la ensalada ee termeeno kon la froota
I sit at the table and "drink" the soup. Next
the salad. And I finish with fruit.

Comer, comer, a mí me gusta comer...

Toda la comida que prepara Mami es tan
deliciosa y tan saludable.
toda la komeeda keh prepara mamee es tan
delees-ee-oosa ee tan saloodableh
All the food that Mommy makes is so
delicious and so healthy.

Comer, comer, a mí me gusta comer.
Comer, comer, a mí me gusta comer.
Comer, comer, a mí me gusta comer...

Desayuno en la mañana. Almuerzo al medio
día.
desayoono en la manyana almwerso al medee-o
dee-a
I eat breakfast in the morning. I eat lunch at noon.

Ceno por la noche. Como tres veces al día.
seno por la noche komo tres beses al dee-a
I eat dinner at night. I eat three times a day.

Comer, comer, a mí me gusta comer...
Tengo hambre, tengo sed.
Tengo ganas de comer.
tengo ambreh tengo sed tengo ganas de komer
I am hungry, I am thirsty. I want to eat.
Tengo hambre, tengo sed. Ya es hora de beber.
tengo ambreh tengo sed ya es ora de beber
I am hungry, I am thirsty. It is time to drink.

Comer, comer, a mí me gusta comer...

Ummm, ¡Qué rico! Mi barriga ya está llena.
ummm keh reeko mee barreega ya está yena
Ummm, this is delicious! My tummy is full.

DIALOGUE

C: Tengo hambre. ¿Qué hay de comer?
tengo ambreh keh ai de komer
I'm hungry. What is there to eat?

S: ¡Yo también tengo hambre!
yo tambyen tengo ambreh
I'm hungry, too!

A: Entonces los dos tienen hambre.
Hay mucha comida.
entonses los dos tyenen ambreh
ai moocha komeeda
Then you are both hungry. There's a lot of food.

¿Quieren frutas? ¿Qué tal una naranja,
una manzana o un durazno?
kyeren frootas keh tal oona naranha
oona mansana o oon doorasno
Do you want some fruit? What about an orange,
an apple, or a peach?

S: ¿Y qué más hay?
ee keh mas ai
And what else is there?

A: ¿Qué te parece un sandwish?
Del qué más te gusta?
keh te pareseh oon sanweesh del keh mas te goosta
What about a sandwich? What else would you like?

S: No quiero un sandwish,
quiero una merienda.
no kyero oon sandweesh kyerooona mereeyenda
I don't want a sandwich, I want a snack.

A: Déjame ver, ¿qué te parece una galleta?
dehameh ber keh te pareseh oona gay-eta
Let me see, what about a cookie?

S: Sí, por favor. Y también tengo sed.
¿Me puedes dar un vaso de leche?
see por fabor y tambyen tengo sed
me puedes dar oon baso de lecheh
Yes, please. And, I'm also thirsty.
Can you give me a glass of milk?

A: Sí, siéntate en la silla a la mesa.
Ya te lo traigo.
see, see-entateh en la seeya a la mesa ya te lo traigo
Yes, sit down in the chair at the table.
I'll bring it to you.

C: Déjame hacerlo, por favor.
dehameh aserlo por fabor
Let me do it, please.

A: Está bien, pero ten cuidado. No lo derrames.
esta byen pero ten kweedado no lo derrames
Alright, but be careful. Don't spill it.

C: ¡Mira, yo lo hice!
meeera yo lo eeseh
Look, I did it!

A: Lo hiciste muy bien.
lo eeseeteh moo-ee byen
You did it very well.

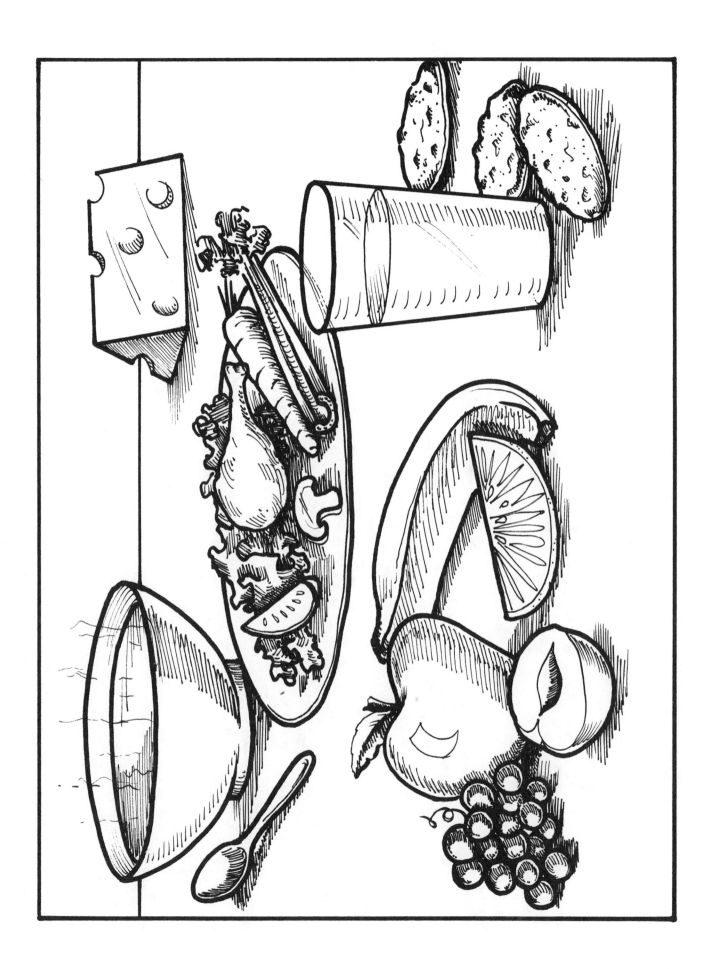

S: **Ummmm. Esto está muy bueno. ¿Me puedes dar otra?**
mmmm esto esta moo-ee bweno me pwedes dar otra
Mmmmm This is very good! Can you give me another?

A: **Ahorita no porque ya vamos a cenar. Dime, ¿les gustan las frutas o las verduras?**
a-oreeta no porkeh ya bamos a senar deemeh les goostan las frootas o las berdooras
Not now because we're going to eat dinner. Tell me, do you like fruit or vegetables?

S: **Me gusta todo, me gustan las frutas, las verduras, queso, carne, fideos, papas y el pescado.**
me goosta todo me goostan las frootas las berdooras keso karneh feedeyos papas ee el peskado
I like everything. I like fruit, vegetables, cheese, meat, spaghetti, potatoes and fish.

C: **Y a mí me gusta la sopa, es deliciosa.**
ee a mee me goosta la sopa es delees-ee-oosa
And for me, I like soup; it's delicious.

A: **¿Ustedes comen de todo, verdad?**
oostedes komen de todo berdad
You eat everything, right?

S: **Yo soy muy fuerte. ¿Y tú, Ana?**
yo soy moo-ee fwerteh ee too ana
I'm very strong. And you, Ana?

A: **Sí, yo también soy fuerte. Quizás ustedes son más fuertes que yo.**
see yo tambyen soy fwerteh keesas oostedes son mas fwertes keh yo
Yes I'm also strong. Maybe you are stronger than I am.

S: **¿Quiéres tocar mis músculos?**
kyeres tokar mees mooskoolos
Do you want to touch my muscles?

A: **Ummmm ¡Tu sí eres fuerte!**
ummmm too see eres fwerteh
Oh! You are strong!

C: **Y yo también soy muy fuerte.**
ee yo tambyen soy moo-ee fwerteh
And I'm also very strong.

A: **¿Díganme, cómo pueden ser tan fuertes?**
deeganmeh komo pweden ser tan fwertes
Tell me, how can you be so strong?

S: **Porque comemos muy bien.**
porkeh komemos moo-ee byen
Because we eat very well.

C: **Sí, comer nos hace fuertes.**
see komer nos aseh fwertes
Yes, eating makes us strong.

ACTIVITIES

Use Spanish expressions, "**¿tienes hambre?**"(are you hungry) "**¿tienes sed?**" (are you thirsty).

Point to foods in picture "**¿qué es esto?**" then ask "**¿te gusta eso?**" or "**¿te gusta la manzana?**"

Just before meal time, sing with your child the Comer/Beber song.

In the kitchen say, "**¿dónde están los fideos?**" or "**¿dónde está el queso?**" etc. (Where are the noodles?) (Where is the cheese?)

Optional object: Basket with real or plastic fruits and vegetables.

VOCABULARY

¡qué rico!
keh reeko
how delicious!

no quiero
no kyero
I don't want

pero
pero
but

déjame ver
dehameh ber
let me see

que más hay
keh mas ai
what else is there?

todo
todo
all (everything)

quiero una galleta, por favor
kyero oona gay-eta, por fabor
I want a cookie, please

díganme (pl.)
deeganmeh
tell me

dime
deemeh
tell me

EL CUERPO

el kwerpo
The Body

Con mi boca puedo hablar.
Con mis oidos puedo escuchar.
Con mis ojos puedo ver.
Con mi nariz puedo oler.
Con mi cabeza puedo pensar.
Y con las manos puedo tocar.
Salto con mis piernas.
Corro con mis pies.
kon mee boka pwedo ablar
kon mees o-eedos pwedo eskoochar
kon mees ohos pwedo ber
kon mee narees pwedo oler
kon mee kabesa pwedo pensar
ee kon las manos pwedo tokar
salto kon mees pee-ernas
korro kon mees pee-es
With my mouth I can speak (talk).
With my ears I can hear.
With my eyes I can see.
With my nose I can smell.
With my head I can think.
With my hands I can touch.
I jump with my legs.
I run with my feet.

Ven aquí conmigo, y canta otra vez.
ben akee konmeego ee kanta otra bes
Come here with me, and sing again.
Con mi boca puedo hablar...

El cuerpo es muy lindo y yo también.
el kwerpo es moo-ee leendo ee yo tambyen
The body is very beautiful and so am I.
El cuerpo es muy lindo y yo también.

El cuerpo es muy lindo y yo también.
Amiguitos, oigan la música, sientan el ritmo. Pues, vamos a bailar.
ameegeetos oyen la mooseeka seeyenten el ritmo pwes bamos a bailar
Friends, listen to the music, feel its rhythm.
Then, we're going to dance.
Pues, vamos a bailar...

Muevan la cabeza. Manos hacia arriba Manos hacia abajo.
mueban la kabesa manos asee-a arreeba manos asee-a abaho
Move your head. Hands up high.
Hands down low.
Vamos a bailar. Vamos a bailar. Pues, vamos a bailar.

DIALOGUE

A: **¡Mira Carmen! Ésta es mi nueva muñeca.**
meera karmen esta es mee nweba moonyeka
Look Carmen! This is my new doll.

Es un regalo de mi abuela. Ella es una muñeca mágica.
es oon regalo de mee abwela eya es oona moonyeka maheeka
She is a gift from my grandma. She is a magic doll.

C: **¿Cómo se llama?**
komo se yama
What is her name?

A: **Ella se llama Lucero.**
eya se yama loosero
Her name is Lucero.

C: **Y ella, ¿qué puede hacer?**
ee eya keh pwede aser
And her, what can she do?

A: **Ella puede hacer muchas cosas.**
eya pwedeh aser moochas kosas
She can do many things.

C: **¿Puede hablar? ¿Puede cantar?**
pwedeh ablar pwedeh kantar
Can she talk? Can she sing?

A: **Sí, ella puede hablar en español y (en) inglés, como tú. Escucha.**
see eya pwede ablar en espanyol ee (en) eengles komo too eskoocha
Yes, she can speak in Spanish and (in) English, like you. Listen.

Muñeca: **Hola, me llamo Lucero. Tengo cinco años. ¿Cuántos años tienes tú?**
ola me yamo loosero tengo seenko anyos kwantos anyos tyenes too
Hi, my name is Lucero. I am five years old. How old are you?

C: **Tengo seis años.**
tengo says anyos
I am six years old.

L: **Yo tengo el pelo rubio. ¿De qué color es tu pelo?**
yo tengo el pelo roobee-o de keh kolor es too pelo
My hair is blond. What color is your hair?

C: **Mi pelo no es rubio, mi pelo es negro.**
mee pelo no es roobee-o mee pelo es negro
My hair is not blond, my hair is black.

L: **Mis ojos son verdes. ¿De qué color son tus ojos?**
mees ohos son berdes de keh kolor son toos ohos
My eyes are green. What color are your eyes?

17

ACTIVITIES

Play Simon Says, using **"manos hacia arriba, abajo,"** **"tócate la nariz"** (touch your nose), **"tócate la cabeza"** (touch your head), etc. Make a dance out of the song. Point to what you are singing about. Point to body part on a doll, say **"¿qué es esto?"** Let your child tell you the word in Spanish.

Optional object: special "magic" doll.

VOCABULARY

muchas cosas
moochas kosas
many things

¡escucha!
eskoocha
listen

ahora
a-ora
now

yo tengo
yo tengo
I have

¿de qué color?
de keh kolor
(of) what color?

muy feliz
moo-ee felees
very happy

C: **Mis ojos son negros.**
mees ohos son negros
My eyes are black.

M: **Tus ojos son lindos.**
toos ohos son leendos
Your eyes are beautiful.

C: **Gracias. Los tuyos también son lindos.**
graseeas los tooyos tambyen son leendos
Thank you. Your eyes are beautiful, too.

M: **Mira, Carmen. Yo puedo caminar sola.**
meera karmen yo pwedo kameenar sola
Look, Carmen. I can walk by myself.

C: **¡Ana! ¡Sus piernas y sus brazos se están moviendo y también su cabeza se está moviendo!**
ana soos pee-ernas ee soos brasos se estan mobeeyendo ee tambyen soo kabesa se esta mobeeyendo
Ana! Her legs and her arms are moving and her head is also moving!

A: **Lucero, aplaude con tus manos así...**
loosero aplowdeh kon tus manos asee
Lucero, clap your hands like this...

Muy bien Lucero, ahora zapatea con tus pies así...
moo-ee byen loosero a-ora sapatea kon toos pee-es asee
Very good Lucero, now tap your feet like this.

C: **Lucero, ¿Puedes escribir tu nombre?**
loosero pwedes eskreeber too nombreh
Lucero, can you write your name?

L: **No puedo. No sé escribir.**
no pwedo no seh escreebeer
I can't. I don't know how to write.

C: **Es fácil. Yo te puedo enseñar.**
es faseel yo te pwedo ensenyar
It's easy. I can teach you.

L: **Me siento muy feliz de estar contigo, Carmen.**
me seeyento moo-ee felees de estar konteego karmen
I feel very happy to be with you, Carmen.

C: **Yo me siento muy feliz también.**
yo me seeyento moo-ee felees tambyen
I feel very happy, too.

L: **Carmen, ¡dame un abrazo!**
karmen dameh oon abraso
Carmen, give me a hug!

C: **Sí, Lucero, me gusta mucho abrazar a las amiguitas como tú.**
see loosero me gusta moocho abrasar a las ameegeetas komo too
Yes, Lucero, I like to hug little friends like you.

L: **Hasta luego, Carmen.**
asta lwego karmen
See you later, Carmen.

C: **Hasta luego, Lucero.**
asta lwego loosero
See you soon, Lucero.

18

LOS ANIMALES
los aneemales
The Animals

En la fiesta de los animales había una vaca y su vaquita.
en la feeyesta de los aneemales abee-a oona baka ee soo bakeeta
At the party for the animals there was a cow and her little cow.

En la fiesta de los animales,
Había un gallo y una gallina.
abee-a oon gayo ee oona gayeena,
There was a rooster and a hen.

Todos cantaban,
todos kantaban
Everyone sang,

Todos reían,
todos re-eeyan
Everyone laughed,

Todos bailaban,
todos bailaban
Everyone danced,

Se divertían,
se deeberteeyan
They had fun,

Era una fiesta feliz.
era oona feeyesta felees
It was a happy party.

En la fiesta de los animales,
había un cochino y su cochina.
abee-a oon kocheeno ee soo kocheena
There was a pig and his lady pig.

En la fiesta de los animales,

Había un pato y su patita.
abee-a oon pato ee soo pateeta
There was a mister duck and his lady duck.

Todos cantaban,
Todos reían,
Todos bailaban,
Se divertían.

Era una fiesta feliz.

La vaca. Gallo. Cochino. Pato.
la baka gayo kocheeno pato
The cow. Rooster. Pig. Duck.

En la fiesta de los animales,
Había un perro y un gatito.
abee-a un perro ee oon gateeto
There was a dog and a kitty.

En la fiesta de los animales,
había un mono y un caballito.
abee-a oon mono ee oon kabayeeto
There was a monkey and a little horse.

Todos cantaban...

Era una fiesta feliz.

Perro. Gatito. Mono. Caballo.
perro gateeto mono kabayo
Dog. Kitty. Monkey. Horse.

En la fiesta de los animales...

DIALOGUE

Ana - Santiago - Rosa

A: **Amigos, hoy vamos a la granja.**
ameegos oy bamos a la granha
Friends, today we're going to the farm.

S: **¡Qué divertido! Gracias Ana. Rosa, ¿Te gustan los animales?**
keh deeverteedo graseeas ana rosa te goostan los aneemales
What fun! Thank you Ana. Rosa, do you like animals?

R: **Sí, me gustan los animales. Pero, ¡no me gustan las culebras! Les tengo miedo.**
see me goostan los aneemales pero no me goostan las koolebras les tengo mee-edo
Yes, I like animals. But, I don't like snakes! I'm afraid of them.

S: **No te preocupes, porque no hay culebras en la granja.**
no te pre-okoopes porkeh no ai koolebras en la granha
Don't worry, because there are no snakes at the farm.

R: **¡Ay! Mira, una vaca, es blanca y negra.**
ai meera oona baka es blanka ee negra
Oh! look a cow, it's white and black.

S: **Mira ese caballo con su potro. ¡Qué lindo!**
meera eseh kabayo kon soo potro keh leendo
Look at that horse with its colt . How cute!

R: **Quiero un caballo.**
kyero oon kabayo
I want a horse.

A: **¡Miren, allá! Los cochinitos con su mamá cochina.**
meeren aya los kocheeneetos kon soo mama kocheena
Look, there! The piglets with their mama pig.

R: **Son todos rosados. Qué lindos, ¿verdad?**
son todos rosados keh leendos berdad
They're all pink. They're cute, aren't they?

19

S: **Una familia de patos.**
oona fameelee-a de patos
A family   of ducks.

R: **Mira allá está la mamá pata y uno, dos, tres, cuatro, cinco patitos ¡Qué bellos!**
meera aya esta la mama pata ee oono dos tres kwatro seenko pateetos   keh beyos
Look, there is the mommy duck and one, two, three, four, five ducklings. How beautiful!

S: **¿Adónde van los patitos con su mamá?**
adondeh ban los pateetos kon soo mama
Where are the ducklings going with their mom?

A: **Se van al agua. Ellos viven en el agua.**
se ban al agua   eyos   beeben en el agwa
They are going to the water.
They live in the water.

S: **Nosotros vivimos en la tierra.**
nosotros beebeemos en la tee-era
We live   on land.

R: **Los pájaros viven en el cielo.**
los paharos beeben en el see-ehlo
The birds live   in the sky.

S: **Y en los árboles, también.**
ee en los arboles tambyen
And in the trees, too.

R: **Y esta música, ¿de dónde viene?**
ee esta mooseeka de dondeh byeneh
And the music, where does it come from?

A: **Hoy es un día muy especial aquí en la granja. Hoy es el cumpleaños del gallo y hay una fiesta.**
oy es oon dee-a moo-ee espeseeal akee en la granha oy es el kompleh-anyos del gayo ee ai una feeyesta
Today is a very special day here on the farm. Today is the rooster's birthday party and there is a party.

S: **¿Y todos los animales vienen a la fiesta?**
ee todos los aneemales   byenen a la feeyesta
And all the animals are coming to the party?

A: **Sí, Santiago.**
see santeeyago
Yes, Santiago.

R: **¿Y los conejos también vendrán a la fiesta?**
ee los konehos tambyen bendran a la feeyesta
And are the rabbits coming to the party, too?

S: **¿Y las gallinas y las ovejas?**
ee las gayeenas ee las obehas
And the chickens and the sheep?

R: **Sí, todos los animales que viven aquí en la granja vendrán a la fiesta. ¡Oigan cómo canta el gallo!**
see todos los aneemales keh beeben akee en la granha bendran a la feeyesta oygan komo kanta el gayo
Yes, all the animals that live here on the farm will come to the party! Listen how the rooster sings!

¡Vamos a celebrar! ¡La fiesta ya empezó!
bamos a selebrar   la feeyesta ya empeso
Let's go and celebrate! The party has begun!

Sí, ¡Vámonos!
see bamonos
Yes, let's go!

ACTIVITIES

Point to animals. Ask "**¿Qué es esto?**" (what is this) and "**¿Qué es eso?**" (what is that).

Recall past vocabulary, **"el muerde,"** (he bites) and **"no muerde"** (he doesn't bite), **"acarícialo"** (pet him) or **"no lo toques"** (don't touch him), etc.

Make animal noises, child repeats and then switch, guessing Spanish names of animals. Reinforce vocabulary outside in a nature setting.

Optional objects: plastic farm animals.

VOCABULARY

Spanish	Pronunciation	English
hoy	*oy*	today
un día muy especial	*oon dee-ya moo-ee espeseeal*	a very special day
no te preocupes	*no te pre-okoopes*	don't worry
vamos a celebrar	*bamos a selebrar*	let's celebrate
una fiesta	*oona feeyesta*	a party
nosotros	*nosotros*	we (our)
no tengo miedo	*no tengo mee-edo*	I'm not afraid
¿tienes miedo?	*tyenes mee-edo*	are you afraid?
no hay	*no ai*	there are (is) no

YO PUEDO. ¿Y TÚ?

yo pwedo ee too
I can. And you?

Miren como bailo. Oigan como canto.
meeran komo bailo   oygan komo kanto
Look how I dance.   Hear how I sing.

Tantas cosas que yo puedo hacer.
tantas kosas keh yo pwedo aser
So many things that I can do!

Puedo dibujar, ir al río a pescar.
pwedo deeboohar eer al reeyo a peskar
I can draw,   go to the river to fish.
Tantas cosas que yo puedo hacer.

**Somos felices y podemos cantar esta
canción y muchas más.**
*somos feleeses ee podemos kantar esta
kanseeyon ee moochas mas*
We are happy and we can sing this
song and many more.
Somos felices y podemos cantar...

Puedo conversar, comer helado y soñar.
pwedo konbersar komer elado ee sonyar
I can converse (talk), eat ice cream and dream.
Tantas cosas que yo puedo hacer.

Te puedo abrazar, dar un beso y saludar.
te pwedo abrasar   dar oon beso ee saloodar
I can hug you,   give a kiss and say "hi".
Tantas cosas que yo puedo hacer.

**Somos felices y podemos cantar esta
canción y muchas más.**
Somos felices y podemos cantar...

**¡Oye, podemos hacer muchas cosas juntos!
Yo puedo hablar. ¿Y Tú?**
*oyeh podemos aser moochas kosas hoontos
yo pwedo ablar ee too*
Listen, there are many things we can do together!
I can speak (talk) And you?

Yo puedo jugar y correr. ¿Y tú?
yo pwedo hoogar ee korrer ee too
I can   play and run.   And you?

**Yo puedo pensar y aprender.
Y sobre todo, ¡podemos cantar!**
*yo pwedo pensar ee aprender
ee sobreh todo podemos kantar*
I can think   and learn.
And above all, we can sing!

**Somos felices y podemos cantar esta can-
ción y muchas más.**

Santiago

**Hola, mi nombre es Santiago. Tengo nueve
años.**
*ola mee nombreh es santeeyago tengo nwebeh
anyos*
Hi! my name is Santiago. I'm nine years old.

**Vivo en un apartamento con mi mamá, mi
papá, mis hermanas y mis hermanos**
*beebo en oon apartamento kon mee mama mee
papa mees ermanas ee mees ermanos*
I live in an apartment with my mom, my
dad, my sisters, and my brothers.

Yo ayudo a mi papá y a mi mamá en la casa.
yo ayoodo a mee papa ee a mee mama en la kasa
I   help   my   dad and and my mom in the house.

Me gusta ayudar.
me goosta ayoodar
I like to help.

Voy a la escuela todos los días.
boy a la eskwela todos los dee-as
I go to school   every day.

Me gusta mucho la escuela.
me goosta moocho la eskwela
I like school a lot.

Me gusta aprender nuevas cosas cada día.
me goosta aprender nuebas kosas kada dee-a
I like   to learn new   things   every day.

**Me gusta comer, pero no me gusta comer
berenjena.**
*me goosta komer pero no me goosta komer
berenhena*
I like to eat, but I don't like to eat eggplant.

**Nado durante el verano, esquío durante el
invierno, me monto en mi bicicleta en el
otoño y vuelo papalotes en la primavera.**
*nado dooranteh el berano   eskeeo dooranteh el
eenbee-erno me monto en mee   beeseekleta en el
otonyo ee bwelo papalotes en la preemabera*
I swim   in the summer,   ski   in the
winter,   ride my bicycle   in the
fall   and fly   kites in the   spring.

ACTIVITIES

Act out the song and reinforce the different
verbs. Have child draw pictures of different
things Carmen and Santiago do.
Ask your child, **"¿qué puedes hacer?"** (keh
pwedes aser) what can you do? Help her to
answer **"puedo correr, puedo cantar."**
Add **"y qué más?"** [and what else (more)].

Optional object: paper and crayons.

MONOLOGUE

Carmen

Hola, mi nombre es Carmen.
ola mee nombreh es karmen
Hi! My name is Carmen.

Tengo seis años.
tengo says anyos
I am six years old.

Vivo en una casa con mi mamá y mi papá.
beebo en oona kasa kon mee mama ee mee papa
I live in a house with my mom and my dad.

Mi mamá me enseña muchas cosas cada día.
mee mama me ensenya moochas kosas kada dee-a
My mommy teaches me many things each day.

Yo ayudo a mi mamá en la cocina.
yo ayoodo a mee mama en la koseena
I help my mother in the kitchen.

Algunas veces, yo preparo el desayuno.
algoonas beses yo preparo el desehoono
Sometimes, I fix breakfast.

También voy a la escuela.
tambyen boy a la eskwela
Also I go to school.

¡Me gusta mucho la escuela!
me goosta moocho la eskwela
I like school a lot!

Mi maestra me enseña nuevas cosas cada día.
mee ma-estra me ensenya nwebas kosas kada dee-a
My teacher teaches me new things each day.
Tengo muchos amiguitos.
tengo moochos ameegeetos
I have many friends.

Puedo saltar a la cuerda muy rápido.
También puedo cantar y puedo bailar.
pwedo saltar a la kwerda moo-ee rapeedo
tambyen pwedo kantar ee pwedo bailar
I can jump rope very fast.
Also, I can sing and can dance.

Juego con mis muñecas y todos mis juguetes.
hwego kon mees moonyekas ee todos mees hoogetes
I play with my dolls and all my toys.

¡No me gustan las culebras!
no me goostan las koolebras
I don't like snakes!

Me gusta colorear con mis creyones y pintar con mi pincel.
me goosta koloreyar kon mees kreyones ee peentar kon mee peensel
I like to color with my crayons and paint with my brush.

Yo puedo hacer muchas cosas.
Yo pwedo aser moochas kosas
I can do many things.

Dime. ¿Tú puedes hacer muchas cosas también?
deemeh too pwedes aser moochas kosas tambyen
Tell me, can you do many things too?

VOCABULARY

soy feliz
soy feelees
I am happy

juntos
hoontos
together

yo ayudo
yo ayoodo
I help

algunas veces
algoonas beses
sometimes

me gusta ayudar
me goosta ayoodar
I like to help

puedo hablar en español
pwedo ablar en espagnyol
I can speak Spanish

mis juguetes
meess hoogetes
my toys

siempre
seeyempreh
always

en la casa
en la kasa
at home

22

BUENAS NOCHES
bwenas noches
Good Night

Buenas noches, amiguitos. Buenas noches, les deseo. Buenas noches, mamá. Buenas noches papá. Buenas noches, abuelito y abuela.

bwenas noches ameegeetoos bwenas noches les dese-o bwenas noches mama bwenas noches papa bwenas noches abweleeto ee abwela.

Good night, little friends. Good night, I wish to you. Good night, Mommy. Good night Daddy. Good night Grandpa and Grandma.

La luna ya salió y las estrellas también. El sol ya se metió. Los animales duermen y yo tengo que dormir también.

la luna ya saleeo ee las estre-yas tambyen el sol ya se meteeo los aneemales dwermen ee yo tengo keh dormeer tambyen.

The moon has already come out and the stars too. The sun already went down. The animals are sleeping and I have to sleep too.

Buenas noches, amiguitos. Buenas noches, les deseo. Buenas noches, mis hermanos. Buenas noches, mi hermana.

bwenas noches ameegeetoos bwenas noches les dese-o bwenas noches mee ermana bwenas noches mees ermanos

Good night, little friends. Good night, I wish to you. Good night my sister, good night my brothers.

En la cama con mi almohada estoy lista para dormir. Y yo cierro mis ojitos esperando dulces sueños.

en la kama kon mee almo-ada estoy leesta para dormeer y yo syerro mees oheetos esperando doolses swenyos

In bed with my pillow I am ready to sleep. I close my eyes and wait for sweet dreams.

La, La, La, La, ...

Buenas noches amiguitos. Buenas noches, les dese-o. Buenas noches, mis muñecas. Buenas noches, mis juguetes.

bwenas noches ameegeetoos bwenas noches les dese-o bwenas noches mees moonyekas bwenas noches mees hoogetes

Good night, little friends. Good night, I wish to you. Good night my dolls. Good night my toys.

La, La, La, La, ...

DIALOGUE

Santiago-Anna

A: **Santiago, es hora de ir a la cama.**
santeeyago es ora de eer a la kama
Santiago, it's time to go to bed.

S: **Ya voy. ¿Dónde está mi piyama?**
ya boy dondeh esta mee peeyama
I'm going. Where are my pyjamas?

A: **Aquí está.**
akee esta
Here they are.

S: **Gracias, Ana. ¿Dónde está mi cepillo de dientes?**
graseeas ana
dondeh esta mee seepeeyo de dee-entes
Thank you, Ana. Where is my toothbrush?

A: **Aquí está tu cepillo de dientes.**
akee esta too sepeeyo de dee-entes
Here is your toothbrush.

S: **¿Y mi pasta de dientes?**
ee mee pasta de dee-entes
And my toothpaste?

A: **Aquí está. No te olvides de lavar las manos y la cara. ¿Tienes los pies limpios?**
akee esta no te olbeeedes de labar las manos ee la kara tyenes los pee-es leempee-os
Here it is. Don't forget to wash your hands and your face. Are your feet clean?

S: **Bueno, no los tengo sucios.**
bweno no los tengo soosee-os
Well, they're not dirty.

A: **Lávatelos de todas maneras. No te olvides de peinarte. Dime, ¿tuviste un buen día?**
labatelos de todas maneras no te olbeedes de paynarteh deemeh toobeeste oon bwen dee-a
Wash them anyway. Don't forget to comb (your hair). Tell me, did you have a good day?

S: **Sí, fue muy divertido. Me encanta cantar y jugar contigo.**
see fweh moo-ee deeberteedo me enkanta kantar ee hoogar konteego
Yes, it was a lot of fun. I love to sing and play with you.

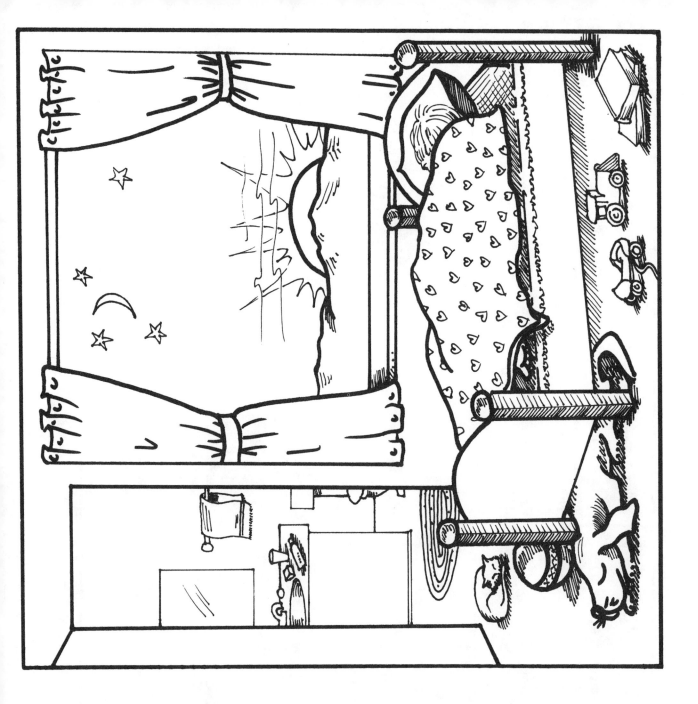

A: A mí también me gusta.
Bueno, ahora da las buenas noches
a todos.
a mee tambyen me goosta
bueno a-ora da las buenas noches
a todos
I like to, also.
Well, now say good night
to everyone.

S: Buenas noches mamá, buenas
noches papá, buenas noches
abuelito, buenas noches abuelita,
buenas noches todos.
buenas noches mama buenas
noches papa buenas noches
abueleeto buenas noches abueleeta
buenas noches todos
Good night Mom,   good night
Dad, good night
Grandfather, good night Grandmother.
Good night everyone.

A: Es tarde. Vete a dormir.
Dulces sueños.
es tardeh beteh a dormeer
doolses swenyos
It's late. Go to sleep.
Sweet dreams.

S: Dulces sueños para ti, también Ana.
Tengo mucho sueño.
Buenas noches.
doolses swenyos para tee tambyen ana
tengo moocho swenyo buenas noches
Sweet dreams to you too, Ana.
I am very sleepy. Good night.

A: Buenas noches. Te veré en la
mañana.   *te bereh en la*
buenas noches   manyana
Good night. I'll see you in the
morning.

24

ACTIVITIES

Lesson 1: Buenos Días

Say **Buenos Días** - point to the object you are greeting. Playfully use different voices. Encourage your child to repeat the sounds and your gestures.

Repeat sentence "**¿como se llama?**" and then fill in with "**se llama _____**" or "**yo me llamo _____**" showing a favorite doll (**una muñeca**) or toy (**un juguete**). Show other photos or pictures and say "**¿qué es eso?**" Then encourage the answer "**es una flor, un globo**," etc.

At every hello and goodbye, say **buenos días, buenas tardes** (good afternoon) or **buenas noches**.

Optional object: toy clown.

Vocabulary:

¿quién es eso?
kyen es eso
what is this?

yo me llamo
yo me llamo
my name is

es muy linda
es moo-ee linda
it's very beautiful

mira
meera
look!

¿cómo se llama?
komo se yama
what's his/her name?

¿cómo te llamas?
komo te yamas
what is your name?

Lesson 2: Gatita

With a real, imaginary or play cat, say "**acaríciala**" (pet her) or "**acarícialo**" (pet him if he's a gatito). "**Ella no muerde**" or "**él no muerde.**" Do the same with other stuffed animals.

You and/or child can pretend to be the kitty or dog and act out the scene of the song and the story.

Give pets (real or imaginary) new Spanish names!

Optional objects: stuffed cat or dog.

Vocabulary:

¿qué tal?
keh tal
how are you?

¡espera!
espera
wait!

ven aquí
ben akee
come here

no te vayas
no te bayas
don't go

¡ten cuidado!
ten kweedado
be careful!

es delicado(a)
es deleekado(a)
it's delicate

¿dónde estás?
dondeh estas
where are you?

¡vámonos!
bamonos
let's go!

suavemente
swabementeh
gently

Lesson 3: La Mariposa

Draw a picture of butterfly wings with your child.
Cut them out to use with the song.
Pantomime song, being a bird, fly, flower.

Point to the picture and identify bee, fly, tree, flower, butterfly.
On nature walks, use Spanish forms for flower, bee, fly, mountains, etc.

Optional object: butterfly wings.

Vocabulary:

¡es tan linda!
es tan leenda
it's beautiful!

¿puedes hacer esto?
pwedes aser esto
can you do this?

¿por qué?
por keh
why?

¡qué divertido!
keh deeberteedo
what fun! or how fun!

no lo se
no lo seh
I don't know

estoy aquí
estoy akee
I'm here

no la (lo) toques
no la (lo) tokes
don't touch it

lo sé
lo seh
I know

¡mira!
meera
look!

26

Lesson 4: El Sapito y la Lluvia

Have child be a frog and then jump, hop and run.
Practice counting to 15 in Spanish with many different objects.
Sing song in bathtub on a rainy day.

Optional object: umbrella or toy frog.

Vocabulary:

no hagas ruido
no agas roo-eedo
don't make noise

yo oigo
yo oygo
I'm listening

está bien
esta byen
okay

sí, lo veo
see, lo bayo
yes, I see it

¿cuántos(as) hay?
kwantas ai
how many are there?

me gusta mucho
me goosta moocho
I like (it) a lot

¿lo ves?
lo bes
do you see it?

me siento muy contento(a)
me seeyento moo-ee kontento
I feel very happy

ven conmigo
ben konmigo
come with me

27

Lesson 5: Arco Iris

Color the rainbow. Repeat colors. Ask "**¿dónde está el rojo, el verde?**" etc. Child responds, "**aquí está el rojo**" or "**¿Qué color es? Es rojo, es verde.**"

Play the wind and change your voices as in the dialogue.

Pantomime other animals using this new vocabulary. For instance, "**¿me puedo montar en tu cola?**" "**No puedes**" or "**Sí, puedes.**"

Reinforce "**es tan lindo**," "**es tan bello**," "**es tan grande**" (big) or "**pequeños**" (small).

Optional object: Picture of rainbow and crayons.

Vocabulary:

tú y yo
too ee yo
you and I (me)

muy cerca
moo-ee serka
very close

siempre
seyempreh
always

es verdad
es berdad
it's true

es peligroso
es peleegroso
it's dangerous

después
despwes
after

muy lejos
moo-ee lehos
very far

hasta luego
asta lwego
so long

antes
antes
before

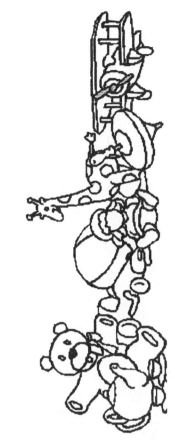

Lesson 10: Buenas Noches

Act out song cuddling child. Have child cuddle a doll and put her to sleep. Play song each night before bed as a ritual. Have child say all the "good nights" in Spanish.

Optional object: familiar stuffed animals and dolls.

Vocabulary.

mira, las estrellas, la luna...
meera, las estre-yas, la luna...
look, the stars, the moon...

mañana
manyana
tomorrow

da las buenas noches
da las bwenas noches
say good night

¿tuviste un buen día?
toobeeste oon bwen dee-a
did you have a good day?

ya voy
ya boy
I'm going

es tarde
es tardeh
it's late

es temprano
es temprano
it's early

dulces sueños
doolses swenyos
sweet dreams

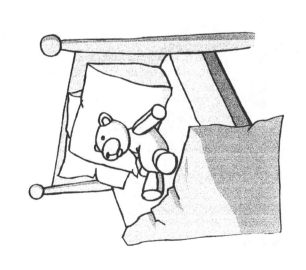

SUPPLEMENTARY VOCABULARY

On Tape 2 Side 2 (**green** label) you will hear vocabulary words with a background of Baroque music. This music has been specially selected and the words are read with specific intonations to affect receptivity and long term memory.

Find a comfortable and quiet place to sit and relax for a few moments. Read along as you listen to the supplementary vocabulary words. Now, rewind the tape. This time, close the workbook and just enjoy the new vocabulary and music. You may even want to close your eyes. The idea is to let the information slide into your memory without any conscious effort to memorize.

During the days that follow, listen to the same vocabulary several times. Be sure and pronounce the words out loud, closely following the speaker's intonation. To avoid monotony and vary the input of the new information into your memory system, use some gestures. Another time make larger movements with each word; on yet another occasion pretend you are an actor preparing an audition for the Teatro Nacional. Experiment with different pitches of voice as well.

If your child or children are in the vicinity, just allow the recording to play without drawing attention to it. You will be surprised to find how well children pick up words and phrases "peripherally."

---

me siento feliz
me seeyento felees
I feel happy

me siento triste
me seeyento treesteh
I feel sad

me siento bien
me seeyento byen
I feel well

me siento mal
me seeyento mal
I feel bad

Terms of Endearment:

mi amor
mee amor
my love

mi vida
mee veeda
my life

me cielo
mee seeyelo
my sky

mi corazón
mee korason
my heart

los niños
los neenyos
little children

niñito
neenyeeto
little boy

niñita
neenyeeta
little girl

mijo	**mi hijo**
meeho	*mee eeho*
my son	my son

mija	**mi hija**
meeha	*mee eeha*
my daughter	my daughter

Temperature/Weather:

hace calor
aseh kalor
it's hot

hace frío
aseh free-o
it's cold

tengo calor
tengo kalor
I am hot

tengo frío
tengo free-o
I am cold

<u>Polite Forms:</u>

perdóneme
perdonemeh
excuse me

con permiso
kon permeeso
excuse me

gracias
graseeas
thank you

de nada
deh nada
you're welcome (lit. it's nothing)
— — — — — — — — — — — — — —

pequeño
pekenyo
small

medio
medee-o
medium

grande
grandeh
large (big)

suave
swabeh
soft

duro
dooro
hard

hasta pronto
asta pronto
see you soon

nos vemos
nos bemos
we'll see each other later (see you later)

hasta mañana
asta manyana
see you tomorrow

<u>Additional Vocabulary (written only):</u>

está caliente
esta kalee-enteh
it's hot

está frio
esta free-o
it's cold (refers to an object)

me siento enfermo(a)
me seeyento enfermo
I feel sick

estás cansado(a)?
estas kansado(a)
are you tired?

me siento cansado(a)
me seeyento kansado(a)
I feel tired

discúlpeme
deskoolpemeh
forgive me

lo siento
lo seeyento
I'm sorry (lit. I feel it)

¡párense!
parenseh
stop! (plural)

¡párate!
parateh
stop! (sing.)

no griten
no greeten
don't yell (plural)

no grites
no greetes
don't yell (sing. fam.)

el cabello
el kabeyo
hair

la cara
la kara
face

la lengua
la lengwa
tongue

el cuello
el cweyo
neck

los hombros
los ombros
shoulders

o = masculine
a = feminine

31

los brazos
los brasos
arms

el pecho
el pecho
chest

el codo
el kodo
elbow

los dedos
los dedos
fingers/toes

la cintura
la seentoora
waist

las uñas
las oonyas
nails

la cadera
la kadera
hips

las piernas
las pee-ernas
legs

el tobillo
el tobeeyo
ankle

él es alto
el es alto
he is tall

ella es baja
eya es baha
she is short

¿qué hay de tomar?
keh ai de tomar
what is there to drink?

hay agua
ai agwa
there is water

hay leche
ai leche
there is milk

el pan
el pan
bread

el cereal
el sereh-al
cereal

Other words for kites:

la cometa
la kometa
the kite

el volantín
el bolanteen
the kite

Keep A Record Of Your Child's Progress

Child's Name _____

Age _____

Date(s) _____

Notes:

OTHER OptimaLearning® Products Available

THE OptimaLearning® Classics

Based on scientific advances in understanding the nature of learning and associated brain functions, the OptimaLearning® Classics will maximize your productivity while reducing your stress. Specially designed by Dr. Ivan Barzakov, one of the world's foremost experts in learning with music, each cassette and CD contains carefully researched classical music with specially sequenced tempos, keys and themes from the great composers.

Each program includes step-by-step written instructions, part of Dr. Barzakov's renowned Optima-Learning® method. These uniquely sequenced arrangements will have a profound effect on your personal and professional life!

You don't have to be musically inclined. Just try them! They will make a difference in your life!

Baroque Music for Learning & Relaxation

(301 & 302) contains excerpts from Pachelbel, Handel, Corelli, Vivaldi, and Albinoni, among others. It is designed to improve memory and comprehension, facilitate test taking and problem solving, enrich teaching or presentations of any kind, speed up convalescence, and aid stress reduction and therapy.

Baroque Music to Empower Learning & Relaxation

(303) contains excerpts from Handel, Bach, and Marcello, among others; the latest and most sophisticated sequences from Baroque composers. It empowers studying, exam preparation, teaching, training, story-telling, stress reduction, convalescing. Especially appropriate for slow movement exercise.

Music for Optimal Performance

(401 & 402) contains excerpts from Vivaldi, Mozart, Rossini, and Bach, among others. It optimizes both mental and physical performance, generates ideas in writing, exam preparation, homework or organizing. It energizes physical exercise, routine work or daily tasks.

Music for Imagination & Creativity

(501 & 502) contains excerpts from Wagner, Ravel, Dvorak, and Berlioz, among others. It stimulates creativity, imagination and intuition. It helps develop visualization abilities, as well as problem solving and decision making skills. Excellent for writing and other artistic endeavors, to gain inspiration and to lift the spirit. It is also very beneficial when used to overcome grief and loss.

Mozart & Baroque Music to Empower Learning & Performance

(601) contains Mozart piano selections, excerpts from Bach, Vivaldi, and Scarlatti. The Mozart sonatas are designed to stimulate mental performance such as planning, analysis, math or computer work. Uniquely sequenced Baroque music empowers studying, test-taking, writing, calming and healing.

LANGUAGES FOR CHILDREN

Your children will love the original songs in these unique language courses. They are especially designed to begin language training with children as young as 2 years old (up to 12).

No previous language experience is required of the parent/caregiver. The new language is spoken and sung by native speakers in both adult and children's voices. The vocabulary of the songs and lively conversations will be learned quickly and soon become a special part of your family's daily routines.

Based entirely on the proven OptimaLearning method, these language courses stimulate giftedness and increase total learning capacities for academic success.

Each course contains two 30-minute audiocassettes or one CD (English for Kids contains one 45 minute cassette or CD) and workbook/activity book. The book gives complete instructions to help the parent/caregiver establish a learning environment that's just right for the child's age and attention span.

Awarded Parent's Choice Approval

SPANISH FOR KIDS
FRENCH FOR KIDS
ENGLISH FOR KIDS

Rated "Best New Foreign Language Resource" by Mary Pride, homeschooling expert and author of The Big Book of Home Learning (Crossway Books, 1990).

LANGUAGES FOR ADULTS

These state-of-the-art courses utilize numerous **accelerated learning techniques** (relaxation, visualization, Baroque music) and provide an excellent foundation for language learning. Learn over 2,000 words and phrases with these home-study courses by Accelerated Learning Systems®. Also excellent for reviewing a language learned in college! The use of a video for visual learners places these courses among the most comprehensive language learning products on the market today.

Each course contains:

- Twelve 60-minute cassettes
- Large format Textbook
- Word Cards and Game
- Physical Learning Video

FRENCH	**ALS 100**
SPANISH	**ALS 200**
GERMAN	**ALS 300**
ITALIAN	**ALS 400**

INSTRUCTIONS IN ENGLISH ONLY

BOOKS

"The Essence and Impact of OptimaLearning®"

This bound collection includes a comprehensive and in-depth report on OptimaLearning, its development and world-wide significance. Features important book excerpts and articles by 25 contributors which illuminate Dr. Barzakov's work in the field of accelerated learning. ©Barzak Educational Institute, Int'l., 1995

The OptimaLearning® Workshop

Special! An illustrated booklet on the world famous OptimaLearning Workshop. Includes models for self-instruction and test-taking in all subjects; techniques for relaxation with optimum concentration; special use of music, optimal classroom teaching, visualization, creativity, and more.
Dr. Barzakov and Charles Gompertz (BEI, 1990)

VIDEO

Reading with Music™ Training Video

Reading with Music (expanded Concert Reading) is a remarkable OptimaLearning technique that helps you understand and remember everything better - facts, formulas, ideas, dry material, vocabulary, anything you need to commit to memory. Use it whenever you need to quickly assimilate complex or technical material. This new knowledge will be easy to retrieve for exams or interviews. Also an excellent technique to enhance teaching and presentations. (48 minutes)
IN ENGLISH ONLY

PROGRAMS AND SERVICES

Ivan Barzakov, Ph.D., addresses today's concern with quality of life through his OptimaLearning® system. By showing people how easily they can incorporate the arts in their lives - at work, in school, with their families - he has helped thousands find greater enjoyment. In these trying times, Dr. Barzakov has been able to assist many in dealing with distress and stress, anxiety and loss, crisis and grief.

Dr. Barzakov shows how creativity and thinking can be enhanced and strengthened by how we approach learning. He demonstrates and discusses OptimaLearning® techniques that dramatically accelerate learning, promote optimum performance, and lead to optimal productivity and reduced stress. The Bulgarian educator who swam seven miles to freedom (see story in **Superlearning**, 2000), also engages his audiences through his storytelling. In his well known inspirational and charismatic style, Barzakov provides useful tips and strategies for immediate application.

Choose one of the following areas or ask Dr. Barzakov about tailoring his presentation to the interests of your group.

- Enhancing Quality of Life Through OptimaLearning® and the Arts
- Liberating Your Mind for Peak Achievement
- Reversing Old Patterns of Learning to Accelerate Memory and Mastery
- Coping with Anxiety, Distress and Crises in Work and Life and Beyond
- Transforming Negative Stress into Positive Energy and Super Productivity

PERSONALIZED CONSULTATION AND COACHING

Memory • Writing Blocks • Creativity • Overcoming Anxiety • Presentation Skills

For the past decade we have provided personalized consultation and coaching either in person or by phone to individuals or small groups of up to three persons.

Dr. Barzakov works with business managers, educators, other professionals, and students. Clients report breakthroughs in creativity, public speaking, writing, work productivity, communications, memory and recall. Remarkable results have been achieved even with a single consultation.

Coping with anxiety, distress, grief, and crises in daily work and life is also an area in which the OptimaLearning system, with its rich interaction with music and the arts, offers rewarding results. Dr. Barzakov works with individuals in this area, often as a complement to therapy.

Pamela Rand, President of OptimaLearning Company, is a Barzak associate and leading OptimaLearning trainer. Her specialty is coaching for performance and public speaking. She is an accomplished actress herself. Author and producer of the OptimaLearning Language for Kids series, she also consults with teachers and parents on language learning for children. Pamela is the mother of three young multilingual children.

Work directly with Ivan Barzakov or Pamela Rand to reach a higher level of excellence in any area of learning, teaching, or performance.

Barzak Educational Institute International
and The OptimaLearning Company
885 Olive Avenue Suite A
Novato, CA 94945 USA
415-898-0013 • 415-898-1654 fax
Email us at: barzak@optimalearning.com
Visit our website: www.optimalearning.com